600g

TRUCKS IN CAMERA

TRUCKS IN CAMERA

E. L. Cornwell

LONDON
IAN ALLAN LTD

First published 1981

ISBN 0 7110 1097 8

Design by Robert C. Wilcockson

© Ian Allan Ltd, 1981

Published by Ian Allan Ltd, Shepperton, Surrey, and printed by Ian Allan Printing Ltd, at their works at Coombelands in Runnymede, England.

Cover photograph by P. J. Davies

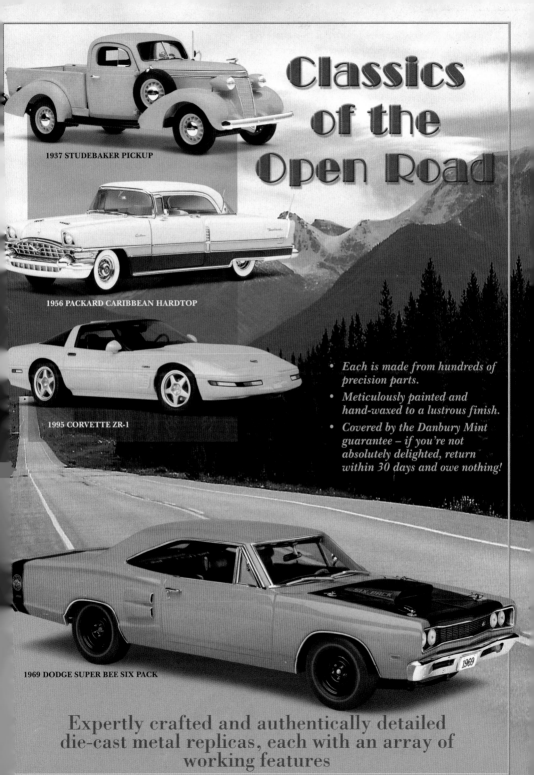

Classics of the Open Road

1937 STUDEBAKER PICKUP

1956 PACKARD CARIBBEAN HARDTOP

1995 CORVETTE ZR-1

1969 DODGE SUPER BEE SIX PACK

- *Each is made from hundreds of precision parts.*
- *Meticulously painted and hand-waxed to a lustrous finish.*
- *Covered by the Danbury Mint guarantee – if you're not absolutely delighted, return within 30 days and owe nothing!*

Expertly crafted and authentically detailed die-cast metal replicas, each with an array of working features

1956 PACKARD CARIBBEAN HARDTOP (ref. PCBH) ▼

In the 1950's, image was everything. In the lofty luxury class, no car deserved the spotlight more than the long, low and parti-coloured Caribbean. Adverts dubbed it "The greatest Packard of them all" and boldly told customers to "Behold the Incomparable."
Actual length is 9¼". (1:24 scale)

£109.80 (*plus £3.80 postage & handling*).

Four monthly instalments of £27.45
(*plus p&h*).

1931 FORD MODEL A PICKUP (ref. FMAP) ▶

It has been said that the Model A 'paved' new roads for a young and flourishing country. With more power and greater speed than its predecessors, the Model A was better suited to the fast-paced lifestyle of the day. Our 1:24 scale model is a stunning replica of an iconic car.
Actual length is 6¾". (1:24 scale)

£109.80 (*plus £3.80 postage & handling*).

Four monthly instalments of £27.45
(*plus p&h*).

1995 CORVETTE ZR-1 (ref. CZR) ▼

A blistering 405 horsepower from its LT5 V-8 engine prop[s] this asphalt-ripping "King of the Hill" 'Vette from 0-60 in le[ss] than 4.5 seconds – and had the looks to match! Our 1:24 s[cale] model is accurate in every detail, from the famous sleek bo[dy] design to fully functional steering and working suspension[.]
Actual length is 7½".

£109.80 (*plus £3.80 postage & handling*).

Four monthly instalments of £27.45 (*plus p&[h]*

▼ 1976 PORSCHE 934 RSR (ref. PRSR)

Throughout the 1970s, Porsche dominated the competition on the racetrack. The magnificent 934 won championships across the globe. This stunning large 1:18 scale die-cast replica pays tribute to one of the greatest Porsches ever made.

Actual length is 9½".

£140 (*plus £5 postage & handling*).

Four monthly instalments of £35 (*plus p&h*).

Large 1:18 scale

1937 STUDEBAKER PICKUP (ref. STUBP) ▼

In 1937, Studebaker surprised and delighted the buying public by introducing its first factory-built pickup. This landmark truck had dashing lines, an all-steel bed floor and a sturdy six-cylinder engine. Our 1:24 scale rendition of this beautiful truck has been crafted from more than 200 precision parts and authentically painted in Chrome Yellow. Actual length is 8".

£109.80 (*plus £3.80 postage & handling*).

Four monthly instalments of £27.45 (*plus p&h*).

1969 DODGE SUPER BEE SIX PACK (ref. SBEE) ▼

In 1969, the year of "muscle car madness", blistering performance at a modest price was the rumble-throated, siren song of the Super Bee. With its incredible triple dual-carbed HEMI® under the bonnet, this no-frills car had one purpose: more bang for buck! Demanding record amounts at car auctions today, this is the definitive "Bee". Our fabulous replica features many operating parts and removable items, including the bonnet and spare tyre. Actual length is 8½" (1:24 scale).

£109.80 (*plus £3.80 postage & handling*).

Four monthly instalments of £27.45 (*plus p&h*).

1967 CHEVROLET CAMARO Z/28 (ref. CZ28)

Combining superior handling and impressive speed from its 302 cubic inch V-8, the Camaro "wowed" customers when it was introduced in 1967. Every aspect of the very first Camaro's racing prowess is here…from the redline tyres and Rallye wheel caps to the "no-frills" interior and fully wired and plumbed, 290hp Z/28 engine. Actual length is 8" (1:24 scale).

£109.80 *(plus £3.80 postage & handling).*

Four monthly instalments of £27.45 *(plus p&h).*

Danbury Mint

Cox Lane, Chessington, Surrey KT9 1SE.

☎ Telephone orders on **0845 218 8000**

Online at: **www.danburymint.co.uk/ins**

ORDER FORM

Danbury Mint, Cox Lane, Chessington, Surrey KT9 1SE

Classics of the Open Road

☎ Telephone orders on **0845 218 8000**

Online at: **www.danburymint.co.uk/ins**

Please accept my order for the classic die-cast replica(s) indicated below:

Ref.	Description of item	Quantity
CZ28	1967 Chevy Camaro Z/28	☐
CZR	1995 Corvette ZR-1	☐
FMAP	1931 Ford Model A Pickup	☐
PCBH	1956 Packard Caribbean Hardtop	☐
PRSR	1976 Porsche 934 RSR	☐
SBEE	1969 Dodge Super Bee Six Pack	☐
STUBP	1937 Studebaker Pickup	☐

When you order more than one item, each will be dispatched separately. If you do not wish to receive mailings from other carefully selected companies, please advise us.
A division of MBI Inc. A company incorporated with limited liability in Delaware, U.S.A.

☐ Please charge the instalments to my credit/debit card.

☐ Mastercard ☐ Delta/Visa

Card No.

☐☐☐☐ ☐☐☐☐ ☐☐☐☐ ☐☐☐☐

Card expiry date _____

Signature _____

☐ I wish to pay by cheque or postal order.
    Please invoice me for the first instalment.

SEND NO MONEY NO

Mr/Mrs/Miss _____
                                    (please print clear

Address _____

_____

_____ Postcode _____

Telephone No. _____

Email _____

XH0

Contents

1 The End of Steam

Foden is one of the great names in commercial vehicle design and construction, and is as old as the industry itself. The company's business was founded on steam and steam-powered vehicles formed its staple product for longer than 30 years, so it is appropriate that this pictorial review opens with a chapter on steam lorries.

Although the advent of the practicable internal-combustion engine really marked the start of the great explosion of road transport in the closing years of the 19th century, steam-powered road haulage had by then been in existence as a practical proposition since at least the middle of that century, held back only by repressive legislation (the notorious Locomotives on Highways – 'Red Flag' – Act of 1861) fired by the vested interests in horse transport and the railways.

After the dead hand of government was partially lifted in 1896, and further eased by the Motor Car Act of 1903, in response to the obvious success other countries were having in the development of motor vehicles, the British commercial vehicle industry gradually emerged from two main sources – from the ranks of the established steam traction engine builders, numbering over a score in the traction engine heyday though fewer than half that number turned to steam wagon manufacture, and from new entrants to the field with petrol-engined vehicles based mostly on designs of continental European origin.

Despite the explosive growth of road transport, particularly after thousands of war-surplus vehicles were thrown onto the market, it was well into the second, perhaps even into the third, decade of the present century before the petrol-engined lorry emerged as a reliable performer with anything like an economic load on trunk routes. Even so, it was really only in Great Britain, with its big lead in steam engine design and production and abundance of low-cost fuel and watering points, that the steam lorry was developed into a highly efficient tool for heavy long-distance haulage. It took the pressures of World War 1 to bring about really substantial improvements in motor lorry performance and reliability, and even then in Britain the steam lorry was preferred for heavy haulage until well into the 1930s and, indeed, until the arrival of the practicable lightweight automotive diesel engine which virtually doubled the amount of useful work extractable from a gallon of liquid fuel. Not until then could the motor lorry compete in overall costs on trunk haulage with its steam-powered counterpart.

After the emancipation of road transport in Britain the Foden company moved rapidly to the forefront of steam lorry development, eventually becoming the world's biggest producer, with a high level of exports, and one of only two companies to stay with steam until its final demise. The business was founded effectively in the 1860s by Edwin Foden when he became partner in the Plant & Hancock engineering shop. In 1880 Foden patented an exceptionally efficient small steam engine which found wide application in industry and agriculture.

Its main attractions were better fuel and water economy than many of its contemporaries and greater compactness derived from the use of high steam pressure, compounding and condensing.

Foden's first important steam traction engine, built in 1887, and many road vehicles that followed, also used the compound engine, but later lorries turned over to simple expansion and superheated steam, generally using two side-by-side cylinders and variable cut-off to make the most of the expansive power of steam. The company originated the so-called overtype wagon, which used a locomotive-type boiler aligned fore-and-aft with the engine mounted on top. The alternative undertype layout generally used a vertical boiler or short horizontal one mounted athwart the chassis and an engine mounted on the frame under the floor.

The company was sometimes criticised for hanging on to the rather cumbersome overtype steamer for too long. It certainly had some disadvantages; in particular the boiler took up too much of the legally permitted chassis length, leaving little space for the body and tending to overload the back axle, and the over-boiler engine could restrict the driver's view, produced a high centre of gravity to the detriment of stability and necessitated a complicated transmission route from the high crankshaft to the axle. In addition the length of the boiler made it more sensitive fo fuel quality than one with shorter tubes and its fore-and-aft alignment affected water level so that the firebox crown could become uncovered when going downhill.

On the other hand, as shown by sales records, for many users advantages outweighed the disadvantages, particularly when supported by Fodens' assiduously preserved high engineering standards. In fact, the advantages were very real and made a substantial contribution to really low total operating costs which, for loads above about five tons, petrol-engined vehicles just could not match. The traditional locomotive-type boiler was very reliable, easily accessible for maintenance and its strength was useful in contributing to overall vehicle strength. The engine was simple and also readily accessible and in the best position to keep heat and steam losses to a minimum. Altogether, the operation and maintenance of the overtype steamer made few calls on high technical skills.

In fact it might perhaps be claimed that the greater skill was needed in firing and driving the early steam wagon to obtain best performance on the road, although rank bad management in either seldom halted a vehicle completely. But efficient working did rely on an intelligint anticipation of power needs and timely attention to the fire and boiler make-up water, skills that became gradually less reliant on unaided human effort as time progressed.

Generally, provided the boiler was properly managed, driving the early steam wagon was simple, control being

exercised almost entirely through the steam regulator once the direction lever was set. Vestigial brakes really only effective for parking (the engine could always be reversed in a real emergency), very low-geared centre-pivot (horse-cart)steering, and a second low gear ratio and differential lock – both selected with the vehicle stationary – to deal with particularly steep gradients or poor traction conditions, were all slow-acting, but matched the comparatively leisurely pace and thin traffic of contemporary life. There was, of course, the regularly recurring need to stop by some roadside stream or pond or other source to replenish water bunkers, apart from coal or coke, though whether that was any more frequent than early ic-engined vehicles' refuelling stops, with smallish gravity-feed tanks usually in the cab, is debatable.

Commercial vehicles powered by both forms of propulsion were advanced rapidly after the war. The pictures in the first section of this book trace the progression of the Foden steamer from the earliest traction engine-derived wagon on steel-rimmed wheels, through the heyday of the overtypes with partially enclosed driving compartments and solid rubber tyres, up to the majestic undertype steam lorry, finally on pneumatic tyres, which formed the backbone of many British heavy-haulage fleets in the early 1930s, until they were driven off the roads by the growing efficiency and greater convenience of the diesel engine, helped in no small measure by discriminatory taxation.

The final manifestation of the road steamer was indeed magnificent, generally much more handsome and always considerably quieter and sweeter smelling than the diesel lorry that mostly replaced it, or the petrol-engined goods

Above: This 1910 Foden 8nhp Showman's Road Locomotive is one of only two built. It was originally owned by Shaw's the Sheffield firm of Amusement Caterers who named it *Prospector.* It is now preserved and owned by Mr Frank Lythgoe of Warburton, Cheshire and shown here at the National Traction Engine Silver Jubilee Rally at Clapham Common, London on 4 June 1977. *S. W. Stevens-Stratten*

Above right: The Foden 1901 wagon built after several false starts from the basic traction engine. The wagon was rated a 3-tonner and could haul a trailer carrying a further two tons. With a full wagon and trailer load of five tons the 1901 wagon won a War Office award for completing a 257-mile mixed trials course without trouble (apart from grounding in a hidden ditch at the end of the final cross-country section) at an overall average speed of just over 6mph. The left-hand driving position with steering wheel under the engine flywheel remained Foden practice for many years.

Right: Although during the first few years some traction engines acquired gripping treads on the driving wheels and rubber bands on the front wheels, basic design and layout remained virtually static throughout a long life. This one, supplied in 1906 to a Scottish agricultural contractor, was repurchased by Fodens in 1956 and restored to take part in the company's centenary celebrations. (1856 was the year Edwin Foden was apprenticed to the firm he later controlled.) *Fodens Ltd*

vehicle for that matter. In overall running costs, including maintenance and depreciation, a steamer of six or seven tons load capacity came out about 25% cheaper than its petrol counterpart and in fact a steam lorry and trailer carrying 12 tons could be operated for about the same overall costs as a petrol-engined seven-tonner.

Top: This 5ton steam lorry supplied about 1910 was still mounted on steel-rimmed wheels and was therefore restricted to a speed of 5mph. Like the first wagon, it had stiff semi-elliptic steel springs but the frame had been moved to inside the wheels and it had additionally acquired a little front-end flexibility through use of a transverse semi-elliptic between the axle beam and the pivoting yoke. Wheel brakes at that time had not progressed beyond horse-cart-type heavy blocks rubbing on the wheeltreads.

Above: The method of springing the front axle is discernible in this picture of a wagon built in 1916 and recently restored to take part in current historic vehicle displays. Although still with only a short body to take its 5ton load, by this time the standard wagon includes rubber-shod cast-steel wheels, entitling travel at up to 12mph, a large contracting-band brake on the end of the rear axle opposite the driving sprocket and some curtain weather protection for the crew. This picture also shows the massive rear-axle radius rod, which was adjustable to take up wear slack in the driving chain, and the traditional one-leg-outside driving position on early Foden steamers.

Top: A new C range of Fodens in 1923 introduced a three-speed gear train, electric lighting as an alternative to standard acetylene head and oil side and tail lights, neat fairings on the rear wheels and internal-expanding wheel brakes in addition to the screw-wheel-controlled band brake. Ackerman steering and the beginnings of real cab protection with right-hand control came a little later. The overtype engine had by the middle 1920s been enclosed and fitted with roller bearings and automatic lubrication but the great length of driving chain necessary with the overtype layout with wheelbase long enough to take a 6ton body is evident.

Above: In the middle 1920s the pressure for increased carrying capacity within ruling axle weights brought the rigid six-wheeler into being, first in petrol-engined vehicles but quickly followed by steam manufacturers. In this 1927 Foden six-wheeler the rear axle was roller-chain driven from the intermediate axle and it had hydraulically operated brakes on the four bogie wheels, with the big contracting band retained on the middle axle as a parking brake. The six-wheeler could take 10/12ton loads.

Left and centre left: The Foden rigid six-wheeler was much in demand for road maintenance, in particular for mechanised tar-spraying. These two pictures show such a machine supplied in 1929 with alternative gravity and pressurised sprays. The mudguards over the nearside rear wheels only, and over the ever-present water replenishment hose, and the 'electrified' oil sidelamps are interesting.

Below: Overtype tractors of the traditional pattern, classified D type, followed the C-type lorry, with such refinements as pneumatic front tyres, Ackerman steering and electric lighting and continued in production by Fodens until about the middle 1930s. These two preserved 40-year olds are demonstrating to rally spectators that even with smooth rubber treads on grass and maximum pull, with differential-lock pins inserted there is little slipping because of the favourable torque/speed characteristics of the steam engine.

Above: For users who needed more body length than was possible with the overtype wagon Fodens introduced its first undertype design in 1927. The new vehicle, classified E type, was of fundamentally different design, with a vertical water-tube boiler supplying superheated steam at 250lb/sq in to a two-cylinder double-acting engine mounted transversely under the frame driving through helical gears and a propeller shaft to a worm-drive back axle. Control of the simple-expansion engine was by a camshaft providing three cut-off (power) positions as well as neutral and reverse. The better balance between the body and 'works' is evident in the 6-tonner illustrated, although there was little if any saving of tare weight over the comparable overtype. *Fodens Ltd*

Right: The new face that Fodens revealed to the world in 1928/9 in the Speed range. It was the company's final production steam design and in general incorporated further developed examples of the undertype main units into a chassis formed of contemporary ic-engined lorry components. It was the first Foden steamer to fit pneumatic tyres as standard and at its most efficient could be worked up fully loaded to speeds around 60mph. *Fodens Ltd*

13

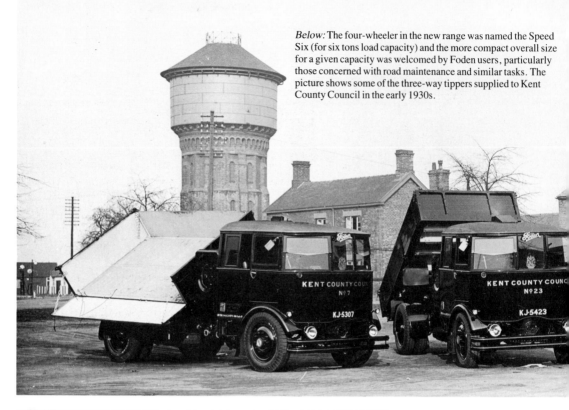

Below: The four-wheeler in the new range was named the Speed Six (for six tons load capacity) and the more compact overall size for a given capacity was welcomed by Foden users, particularly those concerned with road maintenance and similar tasks. The picture shows some of the three-way tippers supplied to Kent County Council in the early 1930s.

Centre left and below left: The six-wheel Speed Twelve was added to the range in 1931. These two pictures show the general layout of underfloor engine, large water tank at rear, spare wheel and the essential water replenishment hose, and two of the beautifully lettered and lined-out body types listed in the maker's catalogue.

Right: Still another body style on the Speed Twelve, and one that was popular with millers and agricultural supply merchants, was the high-sided tipper, in which the water tank was mounted behind the cab. Tipping gear and brakes, both of which had often been powered directly by steam pressure in earlier vehicles, were by this time mostly hydraulically operated. *Fodens Ltd*

15

Above and right: Never-failing attractions at ancient commercial vehicle exhibitions and rallies are the steamers, and most numerous of the steam lorries are Foden overtypes, mostly meticulously restored and eloquent reminders of an early road haulage history that was peculiarly British. These four pictures show Foden overtype steam wagons on the London-Brighton road taking part in the Historic Commercial Vehicle Club's annual run, in the late 1970s. *all W.H.R. Godwin*

2 Into the Diesel Era

Even before the introduction of the final range of Foden steamers the company was studying the possibility of entry into the ic-engined lorry market, though not without considerable dissension among board and management people and eventually a serious split in the Foden family. Despite the dissension, development of petrol- and diesel-engined chassis went ahead, even going down to the lighter end of the market not previously touched by Fodens, using a variety of petrol and diesel engines. Out of those experiments came considerable trouble and financial loss, not least because for the first time the company was having to rely on outsiders for the quality of major components, and users expected the new lightweight vehicles to stand up to the heavy work for which traditional Fodens were noted.

As it turned out there was also good fortune, in one of the numerous engines used during those early experiments. Those using petrol engines soon tailed off and production continued for a few years only for those Foden users who were difficult to convince of the diesel's superiority. Out of the several makes of diesel tried one stood out and when production of diesel-powered chassis started in earnest it was centered around the budding Gardner diesel, the one engine above all others that set standards of reliability, fuel efficiency and longevity always, it proved, just out of reach of the rest of the world's automotive engine manufacturers.

There were automotive-type diesels before Gardner; as far back as 1911 and 1912 Swiss Safir and German MAN compression-ignition engines were being shown in road vehicles in Milan and Berlin but they failed miserably, in no small measure because of the imprecision of Diesel's original form of air-blast fuel injection. It took the end of the war and Robert Bosch's mechanically driven 'jerk'-type pump to give the road transport diesel a fresh start, which became public when a MAN diesel lorry shown in Berlin in 1924 attracted orders from the Bavarian Post Office – and started a trend.

Before long several British commercial vehicle makers started to design diesel engines, mostly around licensed German and Swiss indirect-injection, or pre-chamber, combustion systems, but they were all dropped within a few years in favour of engines employing the direct-injection, or open-chamber, form successfully developed by Gardner in automotive-size engines. Like Cummins in the USA (which came into commercial vehicles in any quantity many years later), the Gardner diesel was originated as a marine engine which by 1929 had been developed into the world's first high-speed cold starting direct-injection engine of acceptable specific power and consistent reliability; in fact, with a high degree of suitability for road vehicle application. Gardner marine engines were fitted experimentally in a bus and a lorry – and started a revolution.

Below: For a period during the economic doldrums of the early 1930s, when steam lorry sales were already under heavy competition from the motor lorry, Fodens experimented with light vehicles even down to the 30cwt and 2ton level. The very lightweights were soon dropped but one of the permanent outcomings was the 4-tonner, which could be fitted with one of several makes of petrol engine, as the radiator badge of this vehicle declares, or with Dorman or (later) Gardner diesel engine.

Above: First fruit of the epoch-making Foden-Gardner co-operation was the 1931 Foden R-type 4/6-tonner. It was powered by a Gardner 5L2 marine engine (fitted with separate heads for each cylinder), a Daimler gearbox and wormdrive rear axle and other components developed from Speed Six steamer units. The gearbox was later replaced with a Foden unit. The vehicle is maintained in running condition by Fodens and has logged a total of nearly 1½ million miles on its largely original engine and major components. The cab was built new in 1956 when Fodens bought the vehicle back from its original purchaser. *Fodens Ltd*

The successful trials and later follow-up by Gardner with engines specifically for automotive application coincided with Fodens' decision to get into the motor lorry market, so it was natural for the two companies to work closely together, in effect to form an informal partnership that has resulted in some of the world's most efficient commercial vehicles and still has a significant influence on goods vehicle design after 50 years.

The first Foden diesel lorry was made known to the public in 1931. It was powered by a Gardner five-cylinder 5L2 engine from the marine range, which although long

and heavy in comparison with contemporary petrol engines perhaps posed fewer problems to Fodens, with long steam experience, than to many companies. The chassis used the rear axle and other components from the Speed Six steam lorry and, since the steamers had needed no change-speed transmission and Fodens had no suitable component, a massive open-top gearbox of Daimler origin that provided eight forward ratios in four-speed/two-speed combination.

The new Foden was classified R type, and it was good. So good in fact that the very first to be delivered clocked up about half a million miles with its original owner, was repurchased by Fodens in 1956 to take part in the company's transport, to accumulate over 1½ million miles before retirement to an honoured place in the company's museum. It still performs regularly in company celebrations and at historic vehicle meetings.

With the next Gardner engine development, the LW range of four-, five- and six-cylinder units designed on more-compact lines specifically for automotive use, continuation of Fodens-Gardner co-operation was assured. The pictures in this chapter illustrate the succession of gradually broadening and improving ranges of Foden diesels that served road haulage in its formative years, during the five years of war, and up to the time of the full return to commercial vehicle production after World War 2.

Left: As can be seen from this picture of another of the first diesels delivered in October 1931, the original cab was considerably more angular, and probably more spartan inside.
Fodens Ltd

Centre left: The Foden diesel's legacy of strong frames and heavy-duty components developed for the steamers meant that there were fewer problems in accommodating high-payload specialist bodies. This 1,750gal paraffin tanker by Thompson Bros (Bilston) was delivered in September 1932.
Fodens Ltd

Below: A short-wheelbase S-type of 1933, mainly designed for tippers but here with platform body, illustrates that it could cope with bulk as well as weight; but this 5ton 6cwt load of straw might well have been a problem on the tree-girt steeply cambered lanes of the early 1930s.

Top: By the end of 1932, with a radiator of higher capacity and taking maximum advantage of the hauling power of the 6LW, a matched lorry and trailer combination found an eager market for payloads of around 11 tons on trunk routes. A common practice on multi-drop journeys was to unload the trailer first and park it, to be picked up again on the return run. *Fodens Ltd*

Above: A new 3/4ton chassis introduced in May 1933 was powered by a four-cylinder Dorman Ricardo diesel engine giving 58bhp at 2,000rpm and four-speed gearbox, with the complete unit mounted in rubber. The petrol-engined equivalent was continued for some time thereafter for users not yet convinced of the merits of the diesel.

Left: A neat if unconventional marriage of steam ancestry and diesel engine and standard lorry cab in a timber tractor exhibited at the Royal Show in July 1935.

Right: Another exhibit at the 1935 Royal Show was this extension of the 6ton range, an S type with a new hydraulic three-way tipper. The chromium nave-plates were to become a longstanding Foden feature.

Centre right: In 1935 Gardner introduced the lighter-weight 4LK diesel engine producing 53bhp at 2,000rpm and Fodens snapped it up to replace the Dorman in the 3/4-tonner and to power a new 5/6-tonner, here pictured with the new 'streamlined' cab at the CV show in November 1935. Unladen weight of chassis and cab was remarkably under three tons.

Below: There was constant demand then, as now, for greater unit capacity to increase the work output of one vehicle and crew, and it was impractical in some industries to do it by drawing a trailer. The multi-axle chassis was the answer, exemplified by this eight-wheel three-way tipper of June 1935 which with Gardner 93bhp/1,550rpm 6LW and eight-speed transmission could legally carry a 13ton payload on the road. The coachbuilt cab designed to blend into the overall lines of the vehicle was called Airstream.

Above: By developing greater flexibility in varying wheelbase length and cutting body weight to a minimum, lorries like this 1936 standard six-wheeler with Gardner 5LW engine could legally carry loads of varying density of net weights up to 12 tons.

Left: As the vehicles themselves became capable there was also a demand for greater speed on trunk routes. By judicious weight trimming, particularly in the special body and the use of the lighter-weight 4LK diesel, this 1936 4-tonner had a tare of less than 2½ tons and could legally travel at 30mph, 10mph more than those with empty weight above 2½ tons.

Below: Another 4LK-powered 4-tonner with a 14ft platform which came comfortably inside the 30mph weight limit and encouraged the initiation of a regular Manchester-London daily service.

Left and below: Two examples of 6LW-powered high-payload six-wheelers, a standard 1936 three-way tipper with high-sided steel-lined timber body for 12ton loads, and a 1937 2,000gal capacity tanker on a chassis fitted with 'big single' rear wheels and tyres. As can be seen, not all Foden users were prepared to accept the exaggerated curvature of the Airstream cab.

Right: An alternative way of catering for bulky loads was this use of a 1937 5LW-powered twin-steer chassis, which could take up to a 10ton payload in the 20ft long van body.

Above left: Meanwhile the standard eight-wheeler had settled down with a works-built 22ft dropside or platform body and a carrying capacity of up to 15 tons.

Centre left: A 1937 example of the popular 4LK-powered S-type 5/6-tonner mounting a special 15ft long body with side roller door, a type much used for deliveries to retail outlets.

Right: This GHT6/50 tractor delivered in 1938 was designed for trailer loads of up to 50 tons, using only the 6LW engine and the alternative underdrive version of the Foden eight-speed transmission and double reduction axles.

Above: The more-powerful 4LW engine was used in heavier four-wheelers (legally 12 tons gross), including this 1937 standard 7½ ton three-way tipper with 11ft high-sided steel-lined body. The Airstream cab appears to have been favoured most for tippers, possibly for the better view it afforded of overhead obstructions.

Right: Fodens introduced the new rationalised DG range at the Commercial Vehicle Exhibition in November 1937; it standardised on Gardner four-, five- and six-cylinder diesel engines and wide commonality of components and brought a big fillip to the company's order book. Here is one of the first DG eight-wheelers, but only a few of the many that followed it emulated the fancy body trim of this show specimen. *Fodens Ltd*

Above: Once having tried Fodens, many users became committed to the make, like the Whittlesey haulier who bought his first Foden in 1934 and by December 1938 owned the 10 vehicles pictured here, which include two of the new DG8s on the left.

Centre left: The standard four-wheeler in the DG range was the DG4/7½ powered by Gardner 4LW; it was available with a choice of wheelbase length to take bodies of various types up to about 16ft long.

Below left: A specialised long-wheelbase tractor from the DG range, a DG6/12 fitted with a powerful winch to aid semitrailer loading, delivered to a Glasgow haulier in August 1939.

Right: An early wartime introduction, in May 1940, designed to provide maximum carrying capacity with economy on three axles was this 5LW-powered (85bhp/1,700rpm) DG5/11 chassis with single-wheeled trailing axle. There were two wheelbases, 12ft 3in or 13ft 1¼in, and chassis weight was about 4¾ tons. Fodens Ltd.

Left and centre left: Travelling showmen were inveterate Foden users from the early steam days and these two pictures of an immaculate generator tractor in service just after the war ended show a sentimental blend of early 1930s wheels and axles with DG cab and radiator expertly faired into the steamlined body. *Both W.H.R. Godwin*

Below: Another early postwar picture, of a DG6 eight-wheel chassis specially reinforced and equipped as a carrier for a Smith of Rodley 12ton capacity crane with 30ft jib.

Top: Quite soon after Fodens got back to a peacetime footing the FG range was announced; here a beautifully lettered and lined 4LW-powered FG4/7½ shows the new concealed-radiator cab at the Scottish Motor Show in November 1949.

Above: And here an FG6/12 six-wheeler is pictured unloading bagged cement onto pallets for shipment at London Docks in September 1950.

Left: A demonstration of the flexibility of the Foden double-drive bogie of an FG6/15 eight-wheeler on the 'colonial' section of the *Modern Transport* test route. With the 102bhp 6LW and five-speed gearbox the fully loaded vehicle had a top speed of 32mph, though legally limited to 20mph in Britain.

Left: An FG6/12 standard dropside lorry in the company's own service transferring an export cargo to shipboard. For several years after WWII a vehicle could be sold on the home market only if an equivalent had been sold overseas. *W.H.R. Godwin*

Below: Missing one front wheel trim but an otherwise smart FG6/15 platform lorry crossing Tower Bridge, London, in June 1950. *W.H.R. Godwin*

Left: The FG eight-wheel chassis provided the base for very high-capacity tippers. Here a new Sparshatts aluminium tipping body weighing only 19¼cwt is shown off at Portsmouth as the first of four being supplied to Southern Gas Board in 1950.

Top: As the advantages became appreciated most manufacturers widened their ranges to include specialised tractors. Here a smart Foden short-wheelbase tractor and matching semitrailer van are pictured in May 1950. *W.H.R. Godwin*

Above and right: The DG range formed the basis of many long-lived specialist vehicles, as illustrated by the Parks of Portsmouth 50ton tractor about to receive its load, and a McAlpine DG6 crane carrier, both photographed in the early 1950s. *Both W.H.R. Godwin*

3 The 1950s and 1960s

The return to free civilian production, after being confined to military vehicles, tanks and shells during the war years, was slow, despite the great shortage of vehicles. Apart from conventional postwar material shortages, a particular constraint on the motor industry was that a new vehicle could only be sold on the home market if a similar one was exported; however, the restriction did some long-term good in ensuring that manufacturers, Fodens included, put maximum effort into renewing old and developing new overseas markets. Return to production of the Gardner-engined DG range, already with a reputation for efficiency and heavy-duty ability, put Fodens into a very strong position in both old and new developing Commonwealth markets.

The period immediately following the end of World War 2 saw other important developments. They included the introduction of the specialised three-axle dumper; the first of the Fodens two-stroke diesel engines which for a number of years made it possible for Fodens to set new and unmatchable standards of gross weight/payload ratios in heavy-duty diesel vehicles; a new two- or three-ratio easy-change epicyclic gearbox which in conjunction with the basic layshaft box could provide up to 12 usable ratios; and the first chassis powered by the new Gardner eight-cylinder 8LW engine. The turn of the decade also saw the emergence of the Series 5 rear-engined bus or coach chassis which, with conventional Series 4 chassis for several years made a major contribution to postwar rehabilitation of the country's rundown passenger vehicle fleets.

During the two decades with which this chapter is concerned, the 1950s and 1960s, the company managed to remain independent while the industry generally was 'consolidating', through amalgamation, takeover or failure, from a total of nearly a score of independent 'heavy' commercial vehicle manufacturers to a total of only half a dozen. Fodens also developed the habit of regularly disconcerting other manufacturers by intoducing one or more pace-setting new features at almost every successive Commercial Motor Show.

The 1952 show innovation was the FE4/8, a four-wheel 12 ton-gross lorry powered by the 84bhp four-cylinder two-stroke diesel engine that was already establishing a high reputation in the marine world. The Foden engine had first been fitted experimentally in a road vehicle in 1947 and much work had gone into both the engine itself, including introduction of the 126bhp FE6 six-cylinder version, to develop characteristics to suit automotive work, and into designing suitable close-ratio multi-speed transmissions. But the adoption of the two-stroke in commercial vehicles even many ardent Foden users resisted on the ground of higher fuel consumption than the Gardner for equivalent work, and they were often supported by their drivers on the grounds of more noise, more gearchanging and lack of the slogging power they had become accustomed to from the Gardner. Many of the same drivers reversed their opinion and clamoured for the two-stroke when they found what a lively performance was there for the taking.

As with many classic arguments, there was truth on both sides of this one and the conflict stemmed from the different basic characteristics of the two engines. The Gardner engine was the epitome of the 'traditional' British automotive diesel, which although governed to a relatively low rpm had flattish torque and fuel curves that varied only a few per cent between just above idling, say 600-700rpm, and governed speed around 1,700-1,800rpm. This gave them the flexible pulling power with freedom from frequent gearchanging and, no matter how well or badly drivers chose to handle a vehicle, the very low fuel consumption for which Gardner engines were renowned.

On the other hand the two-stroke (any two-stroke, but the positively scavenged uniflow system adopted by Fodens is generally the most efficient) is especially sensitive to tuning, largely because for a given rotational speed all phases of charging, combustion and exhausting occur at twice the rate of a fourstroke, and its performance both in torque developed and fuel efficiency is always more peaky than a well-designed four-stroke. Remarkable work was done on the Foden design to broaden the torque output so that it could be slogged by unenterprising drivers, but it proved more difficult to flatten the fuel curve and there remained a disadvantage if the engine was habitually worked too far away from its optimum rpm. In practice it meant that whereas a well-driven FE-powered vehicle could match the Gardner-powered equivalent in work output with hardly any fuel penalty, a driver reluctant to use the gearbox appropriately would come out with varying degrees of adverse, and occasionally disastrous, fuel consumption.

Even so, the two-stroke engine had a direct beneficial effect on Foden design. It was physically much smaller than contemporary four-strokes and its low specific weight particularly allowed unprecedented margins for body and payload within ruling gross weight limits, for example the four-wheel dumptruck with six cubic yards capacity introduced at the 1954 show. It also had an indirect benefit, enjoyed as much by rival manufacturers as by Fodens, in spurring Gardner to do something quickly about the comparatively large mass of the LW engines, which resulted in the incomparable LX series that showed considerable reductions in specific bulk and weight without sacrificing any of the Gardner edge in fuel efficiency, reliability and longevity.

Other advances by Fodens continued, with air brakes and power steering at the 1956 show, a reinforced-plastics cab and a 56,000lb-payload dumper in 1958, followed by the improved Dynamic two-stroke development, the first British production tilt-cab chassis, matched articulated combinations and exceptionally low-height crane-carriers during the 1960s. The further

widening of the Foden range, particularly into the higher
weight levels and higher speeds permitted on motorways,
was made possible by the use of higher-powered
Rolls-Royce and Cummins diesel engines as they became
available, as well as by the power increases achieved by
Gardner in the 6LX series. Sadly, to many, the Foden
two-stroke diesel gradually lost favour, not through any
technical shortcomings but more because low-volume
production meant relatively high cost, and finally was
offered no more in commercial vehicles from the early
1970s.

The pictures in this chapter show a wide cross-section
of the developing range of Foden vehicles and
some of the work they performed during that most
significant two decades of goods vehicle development,
through the heyday of the 24 ton (legal UK) 20mph
eight-wheeler, up to the attainment of the 60mph 40 ton
motorway road train making its massive inroads into the
trunk-haulage business of railways and shipping lines.

Left: Fodens had enjoyed a rather desultory passenger vehicle market since the middle 1930s, with a few stalwart adherents in municipal fleets. The company widened its bus business to cash in on the postwar boom and in 1950 introduced the neat Series 5 rear-engined passenger chassis, powered by its own new two-stroke or Gardner diesel engine, which for several years had customers queueing up. Here one is seen on display at the South Bank, London, exhibition in 1951. *W.H.R. Godwin*

Bottom left: Foden's own diesel engine designed in the middle 1940s and fitted in production vehicles from the early 1950s was a positively scavenged uniflow two-stroke of very low specific weight and bulk. Here a six-cylinder version producing 126bhp at 2,000rpm is pictured at the Turin Motor Show.

Below: An FE6-powered 24ton gross eight-wheeler with Jekta 36cu yd mechanical-discharge body delivered by Walkers & County Cars to BRS in 1951 for bulk haulage of sugar beet pulp.

Bottom: The alternative 24ton gross vehicle at that time, which could also be Foden or Gardner powered, was the artic, typified by this stylish bulk milk tanker delivered in November 1951.

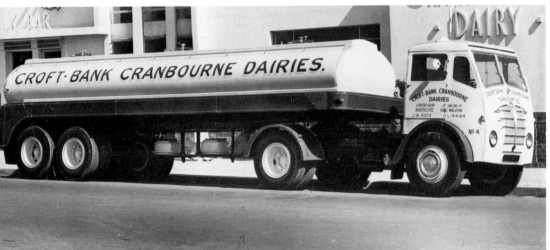

Above right: In the early postwar years the Foden eight-wheeler became the backbone of numerous heavy-haulage fleets, including Drinkwaters which was responsible for disposing of much of London's rubbish. Here one of the company's 10cu yd tippers on FG6/15 chassis is pictured on steep A6 road in St Albans in August 1952. *W.H.R. Godwin*

Centre right: Here a trailer-hauling FG six-wheeler of Motor Packing Company's fleet takes on a load of ckd export tractors for transport to the docks in summer 1952. *W.H.R Godwin*

Below: And here a two-stroke-powered FE6/15 drawing a Homalloy 24ft trailer, also owned by Motor Packing Company, demonstrates mastery over a huge load of docks-bound tractors in May 1953.

Above: An FGTU6/30 tractor carrying a winch and ballast weight, with S18 cab modified to take a bigger radiator and tropics protection, and low-loading trailer for the India Store Department in 1952. The tractor also carried a fifth-wheel coupling so that the trailer could be used as a semi with the dolly removed.

Centre left: Another 1952 export delivery, also with 'tropicalised' cab, was this eight-wheeler to a New South Wales (Australia) quarry, which obviously believed in taking full advantage of the Foden's generous margins of strength.

Below left: Foden chassis were frequently chosen to pioneer new bulk transport developments. Here one of the two bulk refined sugar tankers supplied to Tate & Lyle in 1952 demonstrates its tipping ability, by which it could discharge a 12ton load in 16 minutes compared with about an hour needed for a similar load in bags.

39

Above right: The following year Joseph Rank took delivery on an FG eight-wheeler carrying a Duramin 850cu ft (13½ tons) bulk flour tanker with pneumatic discharger that could deliver the load to a height of 100ft in about 40 minutes.

Centre right: Meanwhile the standard range of Fodens was enjoying a wider popularity than it had ever known. This 1952 Gardner 4LW-powered 12ton gross tipper chassis had a 12ft body with 2ft 3in-high sides. *Fodens Ltd*

Below: And this 6LW-powered eight-wheeler with 20ft platform and headboard joined the big Blue Circle fleet also in 1952.

Left: At any other time this Mowlem's six-wheeler would have been given short shrift in The Mall, where commercial vehicles are not normally permitted, but here it is engaged in erecting decorations for the Coronation in 1953. *W.H.R. Godwin*

Below: A long-wheelbase four-wheeler forms the basis for a coachbuilt confectionery van designed for pallet loads. The bay floor modification helps forklift loading but obviously means a strenuous start for the Foden. *W.H.R. Godwin*

Above: A two-stroke-powered FETU6/30 tractor and pole trailer coping with a 700cu ft (25ton) elm tree in May 1953. *Fodens Ltd*

Centre right: Not a new delivery in 1953, but smart enough to have been, and considered well worth photographing in Coronation year. In fact this 1937 5LW-powered twin-steer DG5/11 had covered 226,000 miles when this picture was taken and the 7/8ton trailer, also built by Fodens, it is hauling was 40 years old.

Below right: The FGD6 dumper was offered for general sale in the early 1950s after several years' development from the FG 12ton tipper built for Steel Company of Wales. Transmission was through Foden eight-speed epicyclic/layshaft gearbox and double-drive double-reduction axles.

42

Left: In 1954 a further developed six-wheel 9cu yd dumper was offered with the Foden FE6 engine as an alternative to the Gardner 6LW and a new half-cab in place of the standard S18 unit.

Below: A stylish new cab (built for Fodens by Bowyer) was not the only noteworthy feature of this FE4/8, here pictured on home ground beside Sandbach Cross during the writer's road test for *Modern Transport* in December 1953. It had the four-cylinder two-stroke engine giving 84bhp at 2,000rpm and eight-speed transmission and carried a full eight tons payload legally; during the test it returned an incredible 15mpg at 23mph average over a fairly difficult route. *E. L. Cornwell*

Above: CAV, always concerned to chart the service performance of its products, chose this good-looking FE4/8 bodied by Maskells for its service fleet in 1954 as a way of keeping a close eye on the fuel-injection equipment, which needed to work about twice as hard as on an equivalent four-stroke.

Right: The FE4/8 was a spirited and efficient performer, but expensive, and most Foden eight-tonner users continued to choose the also efficient but more sedate FG4/7½, like this high-sided lorry used by Liverpool Warehousing on long-distance work. *W.H.R. Godwin*

Below: Staffordshire County Council put this special bodied FG5 weighbridge testing outfit to work in 1955. The loose test weights could be completely loaded or unloaded in less than 10 minutes by the fitted hydraulic lifting gear.

Above right: In 1954 Fodens started regularly to use new chassis designations in which the last figure represented permitted gross weight instead of, as hitherto, notional load capacity. The standard Gardner-powered eight-wheeler, as here shown with special Homalloy 20ft tipping body designed to carry 12 tons of powdered polythene for ICI, was thus an FG6/24.

Below right: In August 1955 Silver Roadways organised the Driver of the Year competition; here one of its own eight-wheelers is pictured taking part in manoeuvring tests during the competition. *W.H.R Godwin*

Above left: First prize for the best-decorated customer's vehicle in a grand procession at the Foden Centenary Weekend in July 1956 went to this immaculate eight-wheeler. *Fodens Ltd*

Left: A very special four-wheeler fitted with the six-cylinder two-stroke engine and four-speed gearbox formed the basis for this Bowyer Brothers 22ft 6in body for Seven-Up bottled products. *Fodens Ltd*

Above: The elegantly bow-fronted S20 cab, first seen in 1954, was gradually extended to the remainder of the range; it looked particularly well on this Duramin Duraflow bulk cement carrier exhibited at the 1956 Commercial Vehicle Show. *Fodens Ltd*

Right: This massive York semitrailer tipper with Pilot hydraulics and Scammell auto coupling drawn by Foden short-wheelbase tractor was one of a range able to take 24-32cu yd. It was first demonstrated in 1957 but UK users had to wait until the gross weight limit of artics was raised in 1964 to 32 tons before full advantage of the huge capacity could be exploited.

Above and Top: The real Foden weight-carriers of the 1950s were the dumpers, which operated mainly off-road, of which there was a broad selection, often matched to the job as the one shown in these two pictures. It is an FGD6 with special side-tipping 23cu yd body built in 1957 to work with a stone-crushing plant 1,400ft up on Penmaenmawr Mountain for the Penmaenmawr & Welsh Granite Company. The vehicle was taken up the mountain in sections and assembled on site.

Left: Here is a standard FG6 dumper, which had the Gardner 6LW engine driving through Foden eight-speed gearbox and double-drive double-reduction axles, with 11.00x22 front and 15.00x20 rear tyres and 10cu yd body – and an illustration of the punishment it was expected to take in everyday use. *Fodens Ltd*

Above: In April 1958 Fodens invited members of the Institute of Quarrying to see its latest dumper, the huge 300bhp FRD6/45, under test over the track used during the war to test Foden-built tanks. *Fodens Ltd*

Left: The Rolls-Royce 300bhp diesel engine selected to power the Foden FRD6/45 dumptruck. *Fodens Ltd*

Below: And the FRD6/45 at work, with a massive 28ton load in a gross weight of 45 tons, given scale by its crew and onlookers. *Fodens Ltd*

Right and below: In 1958 also this Foden FG6/20 formed the basis for an essay into the British muck-shifting business by the Bennes-Marel multi-bucket system, which could set the 10cu yd skip down onto the ground or tip it as shown in the picture below.

Below right: Distinctive Foden styling was advanced a stage farther in 1957 with the S21 cab of glass-reinforced plastics. It was offered as an alternative to the steel unit and after appearing at the 1958 Commercial Vehicle Show it was dubbed the 'Spaceship' or 'Sputnik' cab. *Fodens Ltd*

Left and below: The year 1957 also saw the introduction of a new heavy-haulage tractor, the FGHT8/80 powered by the Gardner eight-cylinder 8LW 150bhp engine and Foden eight-speed transmission. The Sunter tractor has pressings from the earlier S18 cab but the later (1958) Farr tractor, which is pictured hauling a 75ton excavator from Chippenham to Warrington, uses the stylish S20 components.

Left: In 1958 Fodens started a trend with a range of low-height crane or excavator carriers, in three capacities – FC14, 16 and 20 – to take cranes with lift capacities of four to 24 tons. All were three-axle chassis with lockable front suspension and springless bogie beam pivoting on Metalastik spheroidal bushes, but with sidemembers of differing dimensions for the three capacities.

Above: The Foden two-stroke engine was progressively developed and by 1958 the MK III FE6 turned out 150bhp (from only 4.1 litres) and had become very popular, particularly with enterprising drivers. The company undertook still another development of the FE6, for the military, who at that time thought that ability to operate vehicles and equipment on a variety of fuels was worthwhile (and nearly ruined the Chieftain tank in their persistence). Pictured here at the FVRDE in 1959 is an eight-wheeler with FE6 150bhp two-stroke modified to run on grades of fuel from petrol to derv. *W.H.R. Godwin*

Left: In April 1960 the Drinkwater 40-strong fleet of Fodens was joined by this new Powell Duffryn hydraulic hopper/compression-type refuse carrier, here seen as the ram ejects its 10 or 11 tons of rubbish. *Fodens Ltd*

Above: Also delivered in 1960, to Salford City Council, was this FG6/24 fitted with 50cu yd Dempster Dumpmaster hopper-loading refuse carrier.

Below: A Foden eight-wheeler with 24ft platform body here forms the basis for Imperial Chemical Industries experiments with Portolite flexible tanks. This one of rayon-reinforced butyl rubber is carrying 2,000gal of ICI iso-octanol. *ICI Ltd*

Above: The late 1950s and early 1960s were surely the boom years for the Foden eight-wheeler, and particularly so after the Mk IV (Dynamic) development of the FE6 engine, introduced at the 1960 CV Show, produced a 15% improvement in fuel economy in the new K-type chassis. These two refined-sugar tipping tankers, one with S20 steel cab and the other with S21 plastics cab, are fitted with the Mk IV engine.

Below: The competing beet-sugar concern also operated similar vehicles. The large-diameter vertical exhausts on the three vehicles, intended at least partly to reduce the two-stroke's strident blast at street level, are worth noting. *W.H.R. Godwin*

Left: Still another 1960-vintage Foden, this time with high-capacity bulk coke body for North Western Gas Board. The readily variable lamp arrangement possible with the S21 plastics cab can be seen in these three pictures.

Centre left: As with most manufacturers, Fodens invited technical press representatives to conduct their own independent tests on new or developed vehicles. Here a test-loaded K-type six-wheeler with Dynamic Mk IV two-stroke diesel and plastics cab is being put through its paces by the author for *Modern Transport* in early 1961. Here, he is connecting up a chalk-firing magazine used in addition to g-meters, to measure brake performance.

Below: By 1960 the new Gardner 150bhp 6LX diesel engine was through its development and test programmes and available in production vehicles. It powered this long-wheelbase HGTU6/25 export tractor with S20 tropical cab, one of two for Australian Blue Metal, driving through the Foden epicyclic/countershaft 12-speed gearbox. *Fodens Ltd*

Right: The combination of high-torque engines, multi-speed transmissions and exceptionally strong worm-drive axles frequently made Fodens a natural choice for higher-than-average duty. This 6,000gal Pluto refueller, for example, operated at well over 30 tons loaded when the legal road limit was 24 tons gross. The tank was lined with corrosion inhibiting Tanclene paint developed by Docker Brothers.

Below: For a few years between the coming of the thirsty big jets and the completion of pipeline/hydrant systems, airports had to cope with bigger and bigger refuellers. Thompson Bros delivered this 40ton gross monster, the first of the (c)10,000gal Python series in September 1960, using a Foden eight-wheeler as the basis.

Left: Standard chassis also were used extensively for airport refuellers. Here a long-wheelbase FG six-wheel chassis of 1950s vintage mounting a turbine fuel tank of about 2,500gal capacity is pictured still in service at Basle Airport, Switzerland, in 1977. *W.H.R. Godwin*

Top right: The latest developments, including increased protection and uprated axles for higher payload, were incorporated in this standard six-wheel dumper exhibited at the Construction Equipment show in 1961.

Right: Bigger unit loads were the order of the day also for mobile concrete mixers; this Foden-mounted Rapier delivered to Ready Mixed in late 1960 had a capacity of 6cu yd and the drum had a new hydrostatic drive.

Above: Big loads were the reason for this 120ft-long combination too, which also figured in 1961 exports. The FCNHT6 tractors were powered by Cummins 212bhp engines and Foden 12-speed transmissions and the Crane hydraulic-suspension trailer was designed to carry items weighing up to 165 tons up gradients as steep as 1 in 7 for a Malayan hydroelectric scheme.

Left: Among exports in 1961 were these three 4LW-powered FG4/13s with Butterfield 1,500gal tanks for Ghana Electricity Division, the fourth order for such vehicles from that customer. *Fodens Ltd*

Below: Another export and another heavyweight, based on a short-wheelbase eight-wheeler to operate at a gross weight of 41 tons for an Australian dairy in 1962.

Left: Sparshatts built this Thermo King refrigerated van on a long wheelbase eight-wheeler for a Reading slaughterhouse in 1961. The equipment was designed to keep the contents down to the required temperature for as long as two days.

Below left: Fodens and Dyson co-operated in the early 1960s to reduce the tare weight of articulated outfits by close matching of tractor and semitrailer. Here the principle is applied to a machinery carrier for the National Coal Board with a total tare weight of around 12ton to carry loads of up to 30ton.

Right: Australia again, taking full advantage of the Foden's pulling power; for this colossal 'train' designed to 'bridge' an 800-mile gap in the railway system for an Adelaide-Darwin container service. The sleeper cab was no doubt essential. *Australian News & Information Bureau*

Centre right: This 70ton-rated tractor exhibited at the Scottish Motor Show in November 1963, an FETU6/70, was unique in being powered by a diminutive 4.1litre diesel engine, a MkVII turbocharged version of the Foden two-stroke that produced 225bhp at 2,200rpm driving through the Foden 12-speed double-underdrive transmission.

Below: Also introduced in 1963 at the Construction Equipment Exhibition was a further developed version of the established Low Line crane carrier with 21in-deep I-beam mainframe members and a low-height cab that could seat four abreast.

Above: Maximum carrying capacity was the object of this Gloster light-alloy tank mounted on a 150bhp Gardner 6LX-powered eight-wheeler with plastics cab for Wincanton in April 1963. Tare was remarkably under eight tons, to give a carrying capacity of 3,800gal of fuel oil. Later vehicles to the same design went over to the Foden plastics tilt cab.

Left: High capacity plus adequate shell insulation and pressure-tightness were objects in Northern LP-Gas tankers designed to serve a propane space-heating system at Shildon railway workshops in 1965. Here a Foden-hauled outfit is discharging propane into the system's storage tanks. *British Oxygen Co*

Below: An FG6/24 eight-wheeler unloading china clay onto conveyors which lead directly into ships' holds at Par, Cornwall. *English China Clay Group*

Right: Foden long-wheelbase van with 20ft Duramin body and Dyson drawbar trailer with 16ft body designed for pallet loading make a very high-capacity wholesale tea distribution outfit; pictured is the first of three similar delivered to Brooke Bond in 1965. *James Booth Aluminium Ltd*

Above: Exceptional strength without undue weight in this steel-framed oak-boarded body built by Walkers of Watford on Foden FE6/24 chassis for John Mowlem in the early 1960s. The bolsters, which were removable, made it possible to carry steel sections up to 50ft long and the strong floor permitted carriage of heavy equipment between building sites. *B. Walker & Son*

Left: The Commercial Motor Show in 1964 saw the formal introduction of the Foden reinforced-plastics tilt cab, the S34. The picture used to illustrate it is, intentionally, an articulated tractor since 1964 was also the year in which new legislation heralded the virtual demise of the general-purpose eight-wheeler by raising the permitted gross weight of a five-axle vehicle to 32 tons, while that of the four-axle rigid remained at 24 tons.

Top and above: To counter the threat to the eight-wheeler, a mainstay of Fodens' business for many years, in 1964 the company offered an eight-wheeler-and-semitrailer combination designed for a gross weight of 32 tons, but it did not catch on. Here a Dynamic-engined 32ton outfit and the detail of its coupling are shown. *Both W.H.R. Godwin*

Right: The handsome lines of the S34 tilt cab show up well in this picture of one type of 32-tonner that did emerge, a twin-steer three-axle tractor and two-axle semitrailer – in this case a special ICI soda ash carrier equipped with compressed-air discharge that could blow the 20ton load into an overhead silo in about an hour and a quarter. *Imperial Chemical Industries*

65

Above: An alternative five-axle arrangement for 32 tons was provided by this conventional Foden tractor and York Triaxle semitrailer introduced at the 1966 CV show. To rate as a 32-tonner the outermost axles had to be at least 32ft apart. *York Trailer Company*

Left: The contemporary conventional four-axle artic had a gross weight limit of 28 tons. This 1966 Foden-York combination for bulk flour haulage could carry a 17½-ton load within that limit. *York Trailer Company*

Above: Fodens built this special tractor in 1965, with Cummins 220bhp engine driving through Foden 12-speed transmission and 28ton-capacity hub-reduction bogie, to haul the Sheepsbridge Equipment Ltd trailer-mounted 55ton 200ton/hour crusher.

Left: By the late 1960s a fairly high incidence of breakage of the large one-piece windscreen in S34 cabs, and in its non-tilt S36 counterpart, led to introduction of the S39 cab, also in glass-reinforced plastics but with two-pane screen, mainly for tipper chassis. Here a six-wheeler equipped with Powell Duffryn skip-handling equipment, although supplied new in 1975, is fitted with the S39 cab. *Fodens Ltd*

Above: The 1964 regulations by no means finished off the eight-wheelers entirely and they remained in steady demand as high-capacity tippers, like this 1969 version hauling a full load from a development site in the middle 1970s. *W.H.R. Godwin*

Above and right: At the 1968 CV show the steel S50 half-cab was introduced, primarily for dumpers and tippers, but it was offered also on normal chassis with the suggestion that it was quieter and lighter and discouraged the carrying of unauthorised passengers. Both it and the S60 full-width cab of similar design had the opening front panel, but the backward sloping screen was not popular on general haulage vehicles and was soon dropped.

4 Into the 1980s

Through ups and downs, through war and peace, for longer than a century, members of the Foden family had been at the head of Foden affairs, until 1980, into the third generation after the founder Edwin. And since about the turn of the century the Fodens were faithfully supported by successive Twemlows. A truly family business which, despite a setback during the world recession of the middle 1970s that necessitated outside financial help and for a while brought in government money, one that continued until this book was well into production as an independent company to follow its long tradition of designing and building only top-class commercial vehicles.

The period covered by this section, from about 1970 to the present, opens with the start on a huge modernisation and expansion of the Elworth works, which brought in new ferrous and non-ferrous foundries and such advancements as tape-controlled machine tools, computer-aided design and planning, a highly efficient production and assembly complex, and a potential capacity increased about fourfold to 120 vehicles a week. It was marked by substantial orders for military vehicles of several types, the dropping of vehicles from the bottom end of the range, new advanced cab designs in both steel and plastics, specialised motorway service vehicles, and a renewed entry into the passengers vehicle market with a rear-engined double-deck bus.

But the biggest change of all was in, first, the tentative Universal series and then the Fleetmaster range of articulated tractors for international haulage introduced towards the end of 1977. The new designs represented a departure from the Foden practice of manufacturing all its own major components apart from engines by incorporating proprietary units such as Fuller transmissions, Lipe clutches and Rockwell axles to go with high-power Rolls-Royce and Cummins engines, and Motor Panels steel cabs. However, the change of policy by no means signalled a shutdown of Foden design and production, rather a broadening of the company's range by permitting uninhibited mix-and-match specifications designed to serve best the widest possible market.

In fact Foden-made major components continued to predominate in the mainly home-market Haulmaster three-axle and four-axle range which started to reach operators in early 1978, in military vehicles and in the later Super Haulmaster export chassis designed for up to 38 tonnes as a rigid and 65 tonnes as an articulated tractor.

The Fodens plant at Elworth was developed into one of the most modern in the world to produce a more versatile range of heavy-duty vehicles than most of its competitors. The reward at first was increased sales, with profitable trading in the two years 1977-79. In recent years sales have included exports to more than 50 countries, no mean achievement for a small independent company in these days of persuasion that biggest and loudest is best.

Alas! Efficient design and engineering integrity were not enough to ride the slump in sales brought about by the current world-wide depression; 1980 saw the calling-in by the company of a receiver and its eventual sale to the American transport engineering group Paccar. The Elsworth business, renamed Sandbach Engineering, continues to produce and service Foden vehicles and is planning to broaden its output with a range of other engineering products.

The pictures in this section illustrate the very wide range of heavy-duty vehicles in the Foden programme when the final blow fell and cover a fair cross-section of the industries and services that use them.

Below: Despite the economic disadvantages of the rigid 24ton gross eight-wheeler for general haulage, or even the 26-tonner later legalised (with minimum axle spread), some carriers still preferred the better safety record of the rigid vehicle for hazardous loads, as this chemical waste disposal tanker supplied in the early 1970s, which also had built-in safeguards against overloading. *W.H.R. Godwin*

Left: In vogue for several years around the turn of the decade, mainly for general haulage types, was the Motor Panels S40 steel cab first used in the late 1960s, here seen fitted to a Huntons tractor for machinery haulage. *W.H.R. Godwin*

Below left: The S40 cab was also available with a sleeping-berth extension and extra roof protection, as on this heavy-haulage tractor supplied in 1973. *W.H.R. Godwin*

Above and above right: Also introduced in the late 1960s, the S60 cab was also of steel but made by Fodens. The backward-sloping screens of the full-width S60 were not much liked, and the contemporary S50 half-cabs, seen here on two eight-wheelers, were even less popular and few found their way onto the roads. *Both W.H.R. Godwin*

Centre right and below right: Many of the pressings for the S50/S60 cabs, and the windscreen arrangement, remained in use for several years, as seen on these two six-wheel dumpers of the early 1970s with much of the superfluous nearside metal removed. *W.H.R. Godwin; Fodens Ltd*

Above left: In 1972 there was a return to glass-reinforced plastics in the S80 cab, but with built-in extra members to provide crash protection, which had been a ground for criticism of some of the earlier plastics units. This 1973 Cummins-engined four-wheel tractor is coupled to a high-volume Crane Fruehauf semitrailer. *W.H.R. Godwin*

Left: A 1973 double-drive six-wheeler fitted with the new cab, which was quickly applied across the whole Foden range. It had an opening front panel and the radiator could be tilted forward for access for routine servicing and the whole cab could be tilted for major attention. *W.H.R. Godwin*

Above: In 1972 changes in the regulations raised the various weight limits, so that this four-axle artic used for collecting milk from farms could operate at 32 tons gross. *W.H.R. Godwin*

Top left: The same updated regulations reawakened some interest in rigid eight-wheelers for general haulage by raising maximum operating weight from 26 to 30 tons, as this Gardner-powered example of 1975. Careful design was needed with weight distribution to avoid overloading individual axles, hence the forward projection of the S80 cab.

Above left and left: But, as previously since the 1964 gross weight revision, heavy quarry and construction site works were the principal realm of the eight-wheeler, usually with tipper bodies of many types and dimensions to suit the nature of the materials handled up to about 24cu yd and 20 tons load capacity.

Above: Apart from the forward projection on rigid eight-wheelers, there were several variations in the S80 cab, which was generally referred to as the S80/83 series. While very roomy, comfortable and well equipped, in the first of the type it was necessary to use a wheel step-ring to get in and out. In this Mk 2 S80 cab on the Rolls-Royce powered tractor, cut-out steps were provided in the rear corners of the front wings. *British Rail*

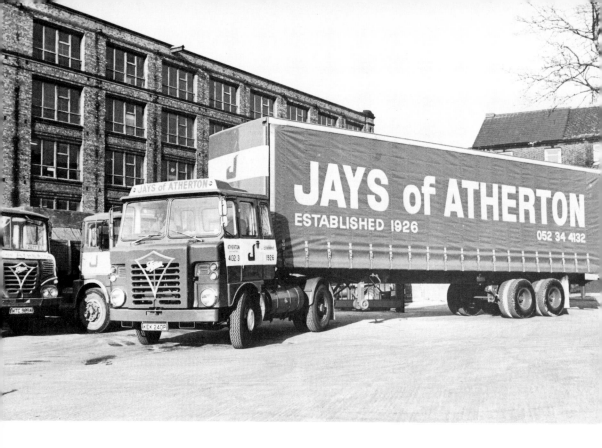

Above left and above: By the middle 1970s the S80/83 face had become a familiar sight on the motorways of Europe and beyond, and an extended sleeping-bunk or extra-crew-seat version of the cab was available, as on these two articulated outfits. *Fodens Ltd; W.H.R. Godwin*

Left: The common haulage workhorse of the period was the two-axle tractor and two-axle semitrailer for up to 32 tons gross weight. Fodens offered a choice of Gardner, Rolls-Royce or Cummins engines and was still unique among heavy-duty vehicle manufacturers in producing a very high proportion of all other components.

Left and below left: Although special-duty tractors like the one above continued in production, vehicles of normal appearance were available for gross weights up to 100 tons. This S80 tractor, with Rolls-Royce 290bhp engine, nine-speed transmission and hub-reduction axles, and King low-loader, supplied in 1974 is rated at 100 tons. *W.H.R. Godwin: Fodens Ltd*

Above: And this two-axle tractor, with the later frontal treatment of the S80/83 cab, and Taskers low-loader supplied in 1976 could operate at up to 60 tons. *W.H.R. Godwin*

Below: A further boost to the 30ton gross eight-wheeler for rough site work was provided when Fodens adopted rubber suspension for the rear bogie. The great flexibility of the Norde system is demonstrated here by a Blue Circle tipper.

Above, centre left and below left: The years 1975 to 1977 were thin ones for commercial vehicle sales, and particularly so for Fodens with generally higher than average prices until the new rationalised production facilities got under way. Even so, many operators obviously shared Fodens' own opinion of its Gardner-powered 30ton eight-wheel tipper, as shown on this 1976 demonstrator and the company moved from loss in 1975-76 to a moderate profit for the following year. The other two eight-wheelers pictured carry a Cravens Homalloy high-sided body for bulk coke and an Edbro body.

Above right: A Cummins-powered 1976 Foden tractor is motive unit for the last Dinosaur skip-handling semitrailer built by Powell Duffryn.

Right: Looking like a throwback with its old S39 plastics cab but actually a new chassis introduced at the 1976 CV Show, the 6LXB-powered Sixer developed especially for site tipper and concrete mixer work, was a remarkably efficient lightweight vehicle. It was new in more than one way as it was the first type to go into production under the company's new policy of much wider use of proprietary components.

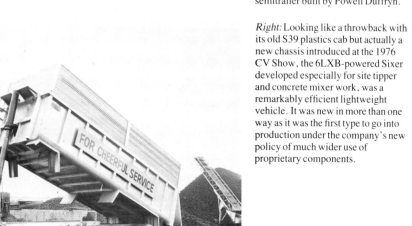

Left: But the beginnings of the new Foden face that led shortly to the current S90/93 cabs also appeared in 1976 applied to a new range of vehicles originally named Universal. This powerful tractor used a Cummins 335bhp engine driving through Foden eight-speed gearbox and hub-reduction axles.

Centre left and below: These two pictures show Foden articulated tractors with S83 cabs and Cummins and Rolls-Royce diesel engines in experiments carried out by the industry and by the Road Research Laboratory in the middle 1970s to produce quieter commercial vehicles. *W.H.R. Godwin; Fodens Ltd*

Right: Fodens' recovery to financial health in the middle 1970s was aided by substantial orders for road maintenance and military vehicles. This Rolls-Royce powered six-wheel snowplough/gritter was built to Department of Transport specification with Atkinson of Clitheroe body. *Fodens Ltd*

Below right: Several types were included in the military orders from 4x4 specialist up to 8x4 plain cargo vehicles. This gun tractor from the 6x6 medium-mobility range also uses a Rolls-Royce diesel – a turbocharged Eagle of 305bhp – with Foden nine-speed gearbox and Kirkstall two-speed transfer gearbox and axles. Its top speed is just short of 70mph and theoretical gradeability fully loaded is 1 in 2. *Fodens Ltd*

Above: The gun tractor has a fitted crane and can carry four Nato standard ammunition pallets and a removable heated and ventilated cabin behind the driver's cab to take an eight-man gun crew. *Fodens Ltd*

Below: Medium mobility in military language means rough cross-country work that would soon stop or wreck the average lorry but the cargo version of the Foden FH70 range is designed to stay in one piece under such conditions while carrying 16 tons and drawing a trailer, as demonstrated in this picture. *Fodens Ltd*

Right: The recovery vehicle in the range is equipped with a 25ton main winch, a 10ton front winch and a lifting beam capable of an 8ton suspended tow. Standard cab for the Foden military vehicles is the current S90 steel unit that provides three stages of accessibility for maintenance – (1) lift-up front panel and swing-forward radiator, (2) cab tilt and (3) cab removal. This wrecker has a crew cab based on the S90 sleeper. *Fodens Ltd*

Left: November 1977 saw full introduction of the new Fleetmaster articulated tractor, and a return to the traditional frontal logo and regular display of the Union Flag on side valences of S90/93 cabs. The cabs are produced both in pressed-steel (by Motor Panels) and moulded plastics on steel spaceframes (by Fodens) and, as can be seen, reverted to a one-piece screen and twin headlamps and introduced built-in foglamps and steps ahead of the front wheels. *Fodens Ltd*

Left: Higher-powered Fleetmasters are also used in the UK for extra-heavy haulage, such as this 290bhp Cummins-engined unit with King low-loader for 45 tonnes gross pictured with a 35ton Foden dumptruck aboard. *W.H.R. Godwin*

Centre left: The S90/93 cab series also includes an extended sleeper version, as seen on this handsome Vallance Transport AR29/38 outfit 'somewhere in Europe'. *Fodens Ltd*

Below: The new S10 sleeper cab introduced in 1979 on Fleetmasters uses a composite steel-frame/moulded plastics shell and one-piece windscreen; it retains the 65-degree tilt angle and fail-safe hydraulic tilt mechanism and is one of only a very few sleeping-berth tractors that can be coupled legally with a 40ft-long semitrailer. This Rolls-Royce 265bhp-powered sleeper Fleetmaster has a total net weight of only 6¼ton. *Fodens Ltd*

Above left: The Fleetmaster represented full implementation of the company's new policy of making wide use of well-proved proprietary major units to take advantage of their universal acceptance by hauliers and widespread service facilities for them. The standard Fleetmaster's gross weight rating of 38 tonnes was set for international haulage, as the UK maximum remained, and remains as this is written, at 32 tons. This AR29/38 (A=Artic tractor, R=Rolls-Royce, 29=290bhp, 38=38 tonnes gross) is used on regular Continental runs. *Fodens Ltd*

Left: Initially offered with either Rolls-Royce or Cummins engines providing from 240 to 290bhp, the Fleetmaster range was extended in 1979 to include the Gardner-powered AG20/33 for 33 tonnes gross and therefore more suitable for the home market. Other main units include a Fuller nine-speed gearbox with R-R and Cummins engines and Foden eight-speed with Gardner, and Rockwell driving axle on all. *Fodens Ltd*

Above: Variation on the S10 theme is seen in this day-cab Fleetmaster AC29/38 with double side windows and two-pane screen. *Fodens Ltd*

Centre right: A pair of Foden AR29/38-York outfits with S10 day cabs pictured while taking part in the *Motor Transport* Project Octave in September 1979 concerned with oil conservation.

Below right: Contemporary with the Fleetmaster, and also taking the S10 day cab is the Haulmaster three-axle and four-axle rigid range intended mainly for the home market. Illustrated is the 6x4 RG20/24 (R=rigid) which has the Gardner 6LXC 201bhp engine, Foden clutch and eight-speed gearbox, Foden rear axles and Foden rubber bogie suspension. *Fodens Ltd*

Above: A Haulmaster RG20/24 undergoing development testing fully loaded in the rough. Conventional taper-leaf four-spring bogies are an alternative to the rubber-spring units and both are designed to stand up to this sort of going. *Fodens Ltd*

Centre left: The Haulmaster is available in three wheelbase lengths, 4,910mm, 5,750mm and 6,350mm – 16ft 1¼in, 18ft 10¼in and 20ft 10in. Here a pair of Gardner-powered tippers are about to start their working lives in a gravel pit in 1980. *Fodens Ltd*

Left: And here a 1980 Haulmaster short-wheelbase MG20/24 (M = mixer) concrete mixer is about to start a busy life with Tarmac. *Fodens Ltd*

91

Left: An addition to the Haulmaster range introduced at the 1979 Scottish Motor Show, this RC21/24 short-wheelbase 6x4 with new Cummins VT504 207bhp/2,800rpm diesel engine, Lipe clutch, Fuller nine-speed gearbox, Rockwell bogie and Foden rubber suspension come out about 2½cwt lighter than the standard counterpart. *Fodens Ltd*

Centre left: The RC21/24 chassis and S10 cab with modified lamp arrangement forms the basis of a new snowplough/gritter with Staffordshire Public Works body introduced at a Hatfield site equipment demonstration in April 1980. Snowplough/gritters are also built on other 6x4 and 8x4 Foden chassis. *Fodens Ltd*

Below: The 30ton gross eight-wheel S10 Haulmaster range includes two wheelbases, 6,508mm and 7,016mm – 21ft 4¼in and 23ft 0¼in – and also offers the choice of rubber or taper-leaf bogie suspension; there is also the option of Gardner 6LXC 201bhp (Type RG20/30) or Rolls-Royce 265L 265bhp (Type RR27/30) engines. Otherwise specification is similar to 6x4 Haulmasters. *Fodens Ltd*

Left: The boom in rigid eight-wheelers that followed the raising of maximum gross weight to 30 tons has been given a further fillip by the Haulmaster 8, particularly for construction work. This rubber-suspension RG20/30, with Edbro aluminium body, is one of over 20 Foden eight-wheelers used by the same Armdale, West Lothian, operator on M8 motorway construction work. *Fodens Ltd*

Below: Another Edbro-bodied RG20/30 owned by a Scottish operator. It is used on clearing foundry waste and on M9 construction work. *Fodens Ltd*

Bottom: And this one, also Gardner-powered, owned by a Sussex operator has a Hydro Hoist tipping body and is used on scrap metal haulage. *W.H.R. Godwin*

Left: This is the FC35A with a full 27cu yd aboard; struck capacity of this one is 22.5cu yd. The standard power pack for hauling this massive gross weight of around 52 tons (53,000kg) is the Cummins C420 380bhp diesel, Allison automatic transmission and Foden double-reduction bogie with differential locks. *Fodens Ltd*

Left: Through the years Fodens has pursued a continuous policy of updating its purpose-built dumpers for operation both within and without legal road gross weight limits. This is a special tractor based on a dumper chassis built for British Steel Corporation to haul a Crane Fruehauf low-loader with molten steel loads of up to 40 tons. *W.H.R. Godwin*

Below far left: The most recent updating of the regular dumper range in 1979 provides four vehicles for payloads of 34,000lb (FC17A), 40,000lb (20A), 54,000lb (27A) and 70,000lb (35A) with standard bodies and Edbro tipping gear. All but the smallest, which has steel springs all round and Foden clutch and 12-speed gearbox, have maintenance-free rubber rear suspension, and automatic transmission. The FC20A with Cummins 280bhp engine and Allison torque converter and automatic gearbox is illustrated. *Fodens Ltd*

Below left: The FC27A has a Cummins 310bhp engine and the Allison transmission; body capacity is 17.6cu yd struck and 21cu yd heaped. *W.H.R. Godwin*

Centre right: In 1978 Fodens introduced the Super Haulmaster series of left-hand-drive six-wheelers mainly for export markets and designed for the considerably higher gross weights permitted in some countries. There are four basic vehicles in the range, two rigids for 26 and 38 tonnes respectively (RC29/26 and RC29/38), and two tractors for 45 and 65 tonnes gross combined weights (AC29/45 and AC29/65). This is an RC29/38 with Edbro body. *Fodens Ltd*

Right: All Super Haulmasters are powered by a Cummins 290bhp engine driving through Foden clutch, eight-speed gearbox and Foden wormdrive axles with differential locks and all have a four-spring fully articulating bogie and S90 steel cab. This RC29/38 carries a new-type Telehoist Monolite body – and shows a certain independence or indecision about the nameplate.

Right: The Road Transport Industry Training Board selected this 1980 Super Haulmaster for training students in driving and heavy-vehicle recovery. The alternative S90 sleeper cab provides increased crew capacity.

Below: This attractively finished AC29/65 Super Haulmaster outfit shows ample length of tractor frame to carry the sleeper cab and massive Carrimore semitrailer, which tells its own impressive legend on the side.

Bottom: No less impressive, though with standard S90 cab and body designed for denser loads, is this Super Haulmaster-Edbro outfit exported to the Middle East in 1978.